Making sense of Russia's invasion of Ukraine

Making sense of Russia's invasion of Ukraine

Paul Le Blanc

Resistance Books

Making sense of Russia's invasion of Ukraine

Paul Le Blanc

Cover design by Adam Di Chiara

Published 2023
Resistance Books, London
info@resistancebooks.org
www.resistancebooks.org

ISBN: 978-1-872242-05-7 (print)
ISBN: 978-1-872242-06-4 (e-book)

An earlier version of *Making sense of Russia's invasion of Ukraine* was first published October 2023 online at https://links.org.au/making-sense-russias-invasion-ukraine.

Paul Le Blanc is Emeritus Professor of History at La Roche University (USA) and author of internationally acclaimed works on the labour and socialist movements, including *Lenin and the Revolutionary Party*, *From Marx to Gramsci*, *Leon Trotsky*, and *Lenin: Responding to Catastrophe, Forging Revolution*. On the editorial board of the Verso Books edition of *The Complete Works of Rosa Luxemburg,* he is co-editor of the second and fifth volumes.

CONTENTS

1. Preface — 3
2. What mistaken friends say – and where they are right — 5
3. Imperialism and illusion — 8
4. Which side are you on? — 15
5. Views of Russian and Ukrainian socialists — 30
6. Lessons from history on self-determination — 39
7. Where the weapons come from — 47

CONTENTS

8 | Notes 53

9 | Chronology of events 77

10 | Ukrainian and solidarity organisations 82

Acknowledgements

I want to thank the following for their assistance in helping/compelling me to think through what is presented here: Jorge Altamira; Ilya Budraitskis; Ana Cristina Carvalhaes; Michael Drohan; Russ Fedorka; Federico Fuentes; Ginny Hildebrand; Harvey Holtz; Flo Menezes; Hanna Perekhoda; Ashley Smith; Mike Taber; Thomas Twiss. These friends and comrades don't necessarily agree with all that I say here (just as they, very much, don't all agree with each other).

Preface

A momentous development is drawing my attention away from the unfolding climate catastrophe on which I have been riveted. The Russian invasion of Ukraine is a major factor fragmenting the left-wing forces which I have hoped would become a major force in the revolutionary struggle for climate justice and human survival. Recently I have met Russians and Ukrainians, and others from Brazil, from Argentina, and from the United States, all making it clear to me that I can't avoid dealing with this issue. I will attempt to do three things:

1. Review what some on the left assert either in favor of the Russian invasion of the Ukraine or against the Ukrainian response.
2. Review Russian and Ukrainian realties and aspects of the war between them.
3. Touch on essential aspects of Ukrainian resistance to the Russian invasion (including where the weapons come from).

In the footnotes I will offer sources that have influenced my analysis, and which I believe may be useful for those seeking to make sense of these realities. But I owe it to readers to indicate my own position at the outset. This is my bottom-line.

- I favor the defeat of Putin's invasion and victory for Ukrainian self-determination.
- I oppose imperialism in all its forms – including Putin's invasion, including NATO.
- I oppose capitalism and favor its replacement with the genuine political and economic democracy of socialism everywhere: the United States, the Ukraine, Russia etc.

2

What mistaken friends say – and where they are right

Some people on the left, for whom I have affection and respect, articulate what appears to be a very clear position rooted in time-tested formulas. What they say goes something like this. We must oppose the horrors of war – and the primary purveyor of those horrors is imperialism, most of all the greatest representative of imperialism on our planet: U.S. multi-national corporations and the government which they dominate. That government reaches for world domination through a foreign policy of "foreign aid" to puppet governments and proxy wars, sometimes subversive activities and sometimes direct military interventions, not to mention the threat of nuclear annihilation. These imperialist policymakers advance alliances – such as the North Atlantic Treaty Organization (NATO). Since its founding, NATO has been employed to advance imperialist interests at the expense of the Soviet Union and – since the Soviet Union's collapse – at the expense of Russia. U.S. imperialism is responsible for the invasion of the Ukraine, which was launched to defend the security of Russia in the face of these threats.

Some of these friends go on to say that they do not favor the invasion of the Ukraine by Vladimir Putin's government – that it was a terrible mistake and should be opposed. However, they do not favor Ukrainians opposing it with weapons. Instead, there should be negotiations.

It might be argued that negotiations under these circumstances (military invasion by Russia coupled with the Ukrainians not fighting back) would result in the Putin government pretty much getting what it wants. For some friends, that's okay. This is because, in their opinion: (a) the Ukrainian government is more or less a cover for U.S. imperialism, (b) the so-called Ukrainian "resistance" is infested with fascist-minded nationalists and murderous neo-Nazis, and (c) the Ukraine is historically part of Russia, not legitimately a sovereign nation.

Not all the friends I refer to hold all positions outlined in the previous few sentences. But all of them do agree on something that I also believe is absolutely correct. We are in agreement on the centrality of imperialism to world politics, and on the need for those who believe in socialism and democracy – rule by the people over our economic and political life – to oppose it.

3

Imperialism and illusion

U.S. imperialism is a reality in our world – and this has been so at least since the 1890s, although it could be argued that it has been a reality since the 1790s. (By *imperialism*, I am referring to military and/or political and/or economic expansion beyond the borders of one's own country, for the purpose of ensuring the well-being of one's economy, including the need to secure markets, raw materials, and investment opportunities.) All too many people in the United States – including some on the Left – seem unclear about this reality, but we can understand neither our history nor the world around us without keeping this clearly in focus.[1]

If that is all we see, however, then we are missing significant realities. I am particularly influenced in my understanding of imperialism by the work (partly complementary, partly divergent) of Vladimir Ilyich Lenin and Rosa Luxemburg. Both saw imperialism as *not* representing a single Evil country, but rather as involving all countries in our epoch – oppressed by competing and contending elites of "great powers" – reflecting the capitalist dynamics of the global economy. Both Lenin and Luxemburg saw imperialism as operating in various ways, depending on the specifics of each country, very much including both the United States and Russia. So it is today.[2]

How this plays out in regard to the Russian-Ukrainian conflict involves multiple components. One of the key instruments of U.S. foreign policy – and what many of us would characterize, therefore, as a key imperialist instrument – is the North Atlantic Treaty Organization (NATO), a military alliance designed in 1949 to contain and push back the threat to capitalist interests represented by the Soviet Union and possible revolutionary insurgencies. Yet another instrument of capitalist expansion and stability has been the European Union (EU).

Both NATO and the EU figure into a shrewd analysis developed by prominent political scientist John Mearsheimer, an influential critic of recent U.S. foreign policy. He asserts that "with the passage of time ... we [policymakers of the U.S.] have moved forward to include Ukraine in the West to make Ukraine a Western bulwark on Russia's border," adding that "this includes more than just NATO expansion. NATO expansion is the heart of the strategy, but it includes EU expansion as well, and it includes turning Ukraine into a pro-American liberal democracy, and, from a Russian perspective, this is an existential threat."[3] This identifies important aspects (although not all aspects) of reality.

Mearsheimer notes that the power elite of the United States has sometimes found itself in a similar situation, and – for example – "overthrew democratically elected leaders in the Western hemisphere during the Cold War because we were unhappy with their policies. This is the way great powers behave." (Of course, "we" are not all part of the power elite – but that is another matter.) More than once, Mearsheimer rejects the label *imperialism*, preferring the term "great power politics" – but for some of us this adds up to essentially the same thing. In any event, he suggests that Putin is in favor of Russia "taking at least the Donbass [Donets Coal Basin], and maybe some more territory and eastern Ukraine, and, number two, he wants to install in Kyiv a pro-Russian government, a government that is attuned to Moscow's interests."

Mearsheimer makes no claims to being any kind of a Marxist or socialist. As we can see, he avoids reference to class divisions and class conflict within countries, blurring all classes together with the governments of their specific countries. Also, he fully accepts the right of "great powers" to insist on having their way. "In an ideal world, it would be wonderful if the Ukrainians were free to choose their own political system and to choose their own foreign policy," he comments. "But in the real world, that is not feasible. The Ukrainians have a vested interest in paying serious attention to what the Russians want from them. They run a grave risk if they alienate the Russians in a fundamental way."

Peace activists Medea Benjamin and Nicholas J.S. Davies represent an orientation and value system that are different from Mearsheimer's. In their substantial effort to make sense of the Russian-Ukraine conflict, however, they repeat a judgment by Noam Chomsky consistent with Mearsheimer's conclusions – that the conflict involves "criminality and stupidity on the Kremlin side, severe provocation on the U.S. side." There is considerable validity to this judgment. Benjamin and Davies go on to pose these questions: "Could Putin really believe that Russia's very existence was under such immediate threat that invasion was the only answer? Could Western leaders really believe that Ukraine's right to join NATO and to reimpose its sovereignty over Donbas and Crimea were causes worthy of jeopardizing millions of lives or risking nuclear war?" They conclude:

Westerners supporting endless shipments of weapons to Ukraine sincerely hoped to defend Ukrainian freedom and sovereignty. But calling on Ukrainians to keep fighting until they won a total victory over Russia and reclaimed Crimea and the Donbas could only lead to massive Ukrainian death and suffering, and a dangerous proxy war between nuclear superpowers that threatened the lives of everyone on Earth.[4]

Benjamin and Davies offer no blueprint for peace, but the implications of what they say would seem to call for a negotiated compromise between the nuclear superpowers, consistent with the "great power" analysis offered by Mearsheimer. Yet their analysis, I think, contains three illusions:

- First, like Mearsheimer, they equate the Putin regime with *Russia* as a whole – but I think this is a terrible illusion.
- Second, they assume (in apparent contrast to Mearsheimer) that Putin exaggerates the threat posed to his regime – but I think his

fear is well-founded and his violent response is understandable.[5]
- Finally, they appear to believe that Ukrainians keep fighting against the invasion because "we" are calling on them to do that – but I think the Ukrainians' commitment to keep fighting isn't the result of anyone egging them on. It comes naturally.

In addition to such illusions, some might argue that there are dubious ethical judgments entwined in their analysis. One is that "we" (or the power elites of Russia and the United States) have the right to decide (or negotiate) what will and what will not happen to millions of others who live in foreign lands. Consistent partisans of actual democracy (not to be confused with pseudo-democratic rhetoric) would disagree. They would insist that people have the right to shape their own future – which implies the right to struggle for self-determination. These matters are explored below.

4

Which side are you on?

I should clarify something. When I refer to friends in this article, I am speaking of those on the Left, those who favor the meaning of the old slogan "Power to the People" – economic and political democracy, a classless society with liberty and justice for all, a society of the free and the equal. Putin is not one of these friends. He is a self-avowed enemy of the Left. His reference-points are not Marx or Luxemburg or Lenin. He has long been prominently associated with the All-Russian Political Party, popularly known as United Russia, which identifies itself as conservative. Nor is he sympathetic to the ideals of Tom Paine or Abraham Lincoln or Frederick Douglass. Although he has sought to maintain a democratic veneer for his rule through what has been dubbed "managed democracy," there is nothing like "rule by the people" in the way his regime functions.[6] Putin is quite openly and quite thoroughly anti-communist, but he explicitly adheres as well to ideologies and philosophies of extreme, authoritarian conservatives long prominent in tsarist Russia. Their ideals were: Orthodoxy, Autocracy, and Nationality. And so are Putin's.[7]

By "Orthodoxy" such ideologists referred to the dominance of the Russian Orthodox Church. By "Autocracy" they referred to a despotic regime not tolerating challenges to its authority (for several centuries this was the tsarist monarchy), making use of brutally violent Cossacks and other repressive forces to intimidate critics and crush all serious dissent. By "Nationality" they referred to the aggressive domination of a vast empire (dissenters dubbed it "a prison-house of nations") in which all ethnic groups were to abandon their

MAKING SENSE OF RUSSIA'S INVASION OF UKRAINE

own distinctive cultures and languages, adopting instead those of a unified Great Russia.

Analysts have pointed to various extreme right-wing theorists – such as Vladislav Surkov and Alexander Dugin, and a long-dead reactionary named Ivan Ilyin – who have directly influenced Putin's thinking and policies, and whose extreme nationalism seems to bend toward a Russian version of fascism. Others have argued that this is overstated. But there is no denying that Putin's political thinking and policies are very much on the right-end (definitely not the left) of the political spectrum. It is also clear – when one considers Putin's more elaborate explanations for the invasion of Ukraine – that a key factor for him is not simply defending Russia from possible NATO incursions (the thrust of shorter explanations) but rather what Lenin would have referred to as "Great Russian chauvinism," the argument that the Ukraine is historically inseparable from Russia.[8]

Many people – including some on the Left – seem unclear about this reality, sometimes blurring Putin's regime together with the self-described left-wing regimes of the Soviet era. Vladimir Putin has never pretended to be the head of a left-wing regime. He is actually part of a right-wing authoritarian trend, often with a populist veneer, that has become all too common in today's world. Regarding Putin's invasion of Ukraine, Russian socialist Ilya Butraitskis warns: "A victory for Putin would strengthen other reactionaries like Trump and the far right as a whole."[9]

There is another point that we must be clear on: the pervasiveness of capitalism in world politics. Capitalism certainly dominates the United States, but it also dominates the world. The end of the Cold War and the triumph of "globalization" has made this more true than ever. And in more ways than one, it is inseparable from the Russia-Ukraine conflict. With the collapse of the Soviet Union, a somewhat similar variant of capitalism became dominant in both Russia and the Ukraine. The economy of each has been privatized, giving rise to domination by self-interested economic oligarchs, combined with breath-taking corruption and soaring inequality, at the expense of the great majority of Russians and Ukrainians.[10]

Capitalism assumes different forms in different

times and places. The hybrid of tsarist capitalism in the Russia of 1914, for example, was not the same as the modern industrial capitalism in the United States during the same period. For that matter, differences can be found between the form that post-Soviet oligarchic capitalism assumes in Russia and in the Ukraine. Both were initially governed by prominent ex-Communist Party functionaries who embraced capitalism and worked intimately with the new layer of capitalist oligarchs – Boris Yeltsin (Russia) and Leonid Kravchuk (Ukraine). Both found themselves challenged, in their inegalitarian and corrupt policies of capitalist transition, by the semi-democratic parliaments established in the wake of Communism's collapse. With support from the army, Yeltsin rode roughshod over Russia's parliament. He ordered it, finally, to be physically assaulted and dissolved, pushing through a new constitution that created an authoritarian executive branch of government enabling him to rule by decree. Ukrainian historian Serhii Plokhy notes that Yeltsin thereby paved the way for "Russia's road to autocracy." In the Ukraine, on the other hand, "Kravchuk never wrested from parliament the right to rule by decree."[11]

Kravchuk was the first President of an independent Ukraine but was shunted aside in a jumble of competing power-players. A major political divide soon developed over whether Ukraine should be more closely aligned with Russia or with Western Europe and the United States. Through the 2014 mass mobilizations in Kyiv's central square (*Maidan*), the so-called or "Euromaidan Revolution," Ukraine's political-economic alignment shifted decisively to "the West." But all fractions of the political elite have been committed to Ukraine's transition to the market economy, and as analyst Renfrey Clarke has noted:

> For Ukraine, the return of capitalism has been a disaster. The country's economic and political elites have seized on the opportunities for self-enrichment furnished by private property and the market, creating a system that is both dysfunctional and at the same time extraordinarily resistant to change. Nor has the fiasco been turned around by

the "Euromaidan Revolution", whose fifth anniversary Ukrainians celebrated— with varying degrees of enthusiasm — in February 2019.[12]

In Russia too, Yeltsin's regime spelled disaster for the Russian people. Yet the authoritarian measures he implemented in the early 1990s provided political tools for his more capable successor who took over in 2000. "Putin and his collaborators pulled the Russian state out of the chaos of the 1990s and centralized it," notes Simon Pirani. "They moved against the Yeltsin-era oligarchs in the interests of the property-owning class as a whole."[13] Despite a partially veiled but soaring inequality, living standards for masses of Russians thereby improved. Of course, to maintain the system's stability, Putin's ideological and political orientation – as we have seen – pulled in an increasingly authoritarian direction.

Yuliya Yurchenko shares a different story regarding Ukrainian capitalism. While referring to Ukrainian politics being dominated by an "authoritarian neoliberal kleptocracy," what she describes seems similar to what existed in Yeltin's Russia, before Putin took control. She notes:

> The combination of ill-prescribed market transition reforms, loaned funds mismanagement and misappropriation by the kleptocratic ruling bloc have resulted in a toxic debt dependency that has become a tool for manipulation in the renewed geopolitical confrontation between Russia and the USA/EU.[14]

Yurchenko insists that we cannot understand what is happening unless we place events within the framework of "the most resilient empire in modern history [which] has not fallen with the fading of the European empires but has grown stronger – the empire of (transnationalising) capital." She adds: "Where empires spread, blood is shed. Blood has been shed continuously across the globe in the name of struggles for further accumulation of capital."[15]

The details and specifics of the Russian invasion of the Ukraine go beyond the framework of this short essay.[16] Just as "who was the aggressor" was beside the point as the First World War exploded in 1914, so "which side should we support" can be a misleading question in regard to the Russo-Ukrainian War – *that is, if we restrict our attention to governments which deserve no support from revolutionaries.*

The Ukraine's President Volodymyr Zelensky – like Putin – is not one of us, is not on our side, is not on the side of the working people of the Ukraine or anywhere else. The assessment of Social Movement activist Vladyslav Starodubtsev is shared by many Ukrainian socialists:

> Even before the war, this has been one of the most popular governments Ukraine has had — which is not saying anything good about it, it was just not as awful as the previous ones. Zelensky's party, Servant of the People, has become the most progressive party in parliament on social issues such as LGBTQ rights, opposing violence against women, and so on. But most of these policies have been promoted with European

> integration in mind, and not because the party is itself progressive.
>
> On the economic front, Zelensky's party is absolutely neoliberal; it has a market fundamentalist orientation. And this war has provided it with the opportunity of a lifetime to push through every unpopular legislation they have ever dreamed of. The war has given them carte blanche to do whatever they want. For example, they have adopted completely neoliberal legislation to deregulate labour relations, which has weakened the power of collective labour contracts and trade unions. Due to their market fundamentalist outlook, they view trade unions and any form of economic democracy as harmful to economic development and see a need to destroy unions.[17]

Social Movement chairperson Vitaliy Dudin makes an interesting link: "a lot of Ukrainian workers are joining the army. We should arm them, so that they can return to their homes alive and empowered to continue the class war against greedy oligarchs." Nataliya Levytska, of the Mineworkers Union and the Confederation of Free Trade Unions of Ukraine, explains: "Prior to the invasion, Ukrainian trade unions fought for wage increases and better working conditions and demanded the implementation of international labor standards. We confronted several attempts to undermine workers' and union rights. Thanks to campaigns, protest actions and negotiations with the government, we stopped those attacks."[18]

Hanna Perekhoda also links resistance against the Russian invasion with resistance to the conservative neo-liberalism of the Zelensky regime. "As Ukrainian socialists, we are demanding all the military, financial, and diplomatic aid we need to win. At the same time, we are organizing against our own government's attempt to dismantle labor laws and push through neoliberal reforms." Attention is given to what comes after the war: "We are also working to make sure that postwar reconstruction serves the interests of workers and oppressed peoples, not the corporations, oligarchs, and international financial institutions like the IMF and World Bank. As part of that, we are calling for the cancellation of Ukraine's odious debt." She concludes: "The needs of ordinary Ukrainians, who keep everything from hospitals to schools functioning and are fighting on the frontlines, must be at the center of reconstruction. The liberated country must meet the demands of the vast majority for justice, democracy, and equality."[19]

There are other issues that must be considered. Fascists and neo-Nazis are brutally inserting themselves into this conflict. That is, in fact, a global phenomenon at this moment in world history. Open neo-Nazis are visible but also (at present) relatively marginal among Ukrainians and Russians alike. Yet it can be argued that there are more numerous authoritarian and extreme nationalist influences among combatants, supporters and even some government officials bearing a resemblance to fascist movements of the past. The Russian-Ukraine conflict is likely to strengthen such fascist elements in both countries. "Both sides accuse the other side of being fascist, but I think that neither side is fascist," notes Russian dissident Boris Kagarlitsky. "That said, the ideology of the far right, and the tendencies that are typical of right-wing populism, and even fascism, are present in both countries."[20]

However, what is especially pronounced in Russia is an incredibly deep feeling and pride among very broad layers of the population about the Soviet Union's central role in fighting against and defeating the Nazi onslaught during the Second World War. "We have," Putin noted in a 2012 speech, "an immense moral right: to defend our positions in a fundamental and lasting way. Because our country was the one subjected to the bulk of the Nazi offensive ... and it was our country that offered freedom to the peoples of the whole world." There is a keen sense of the horrific sacrifices (more than 20 million Soviet dead out of a population of 200 million) during the Great Patriotic War. This plays a central role in government discussions of, and efforts to rally popular support for, the Russian-Ukrainian conflict. That parallel has not, however, gained universal acceptance within Russia – and among a significant number of Russians there has been open opposition to the war. The result has been fierce government repression, which some dissident Russians suggest has itself become a sort of fascism. More than this, however, there has also been a significant growth of far-right organizations and currents in Putin's Russia, closely allied with the Putin regime and its war in Ukraine.[21]

While not as severe as in Russia, Ukraine's Zelensky government also employs repression against opponents of the war. This includes Yurii Sheliazhenko, Executive Secretary of the Ukrainian Pacifist Movement. His organization adopted a statement that said:

> Peace, not war, is the norm of human life. War is an organized mass murder. Our sacred duty is that we shall not kill. ... Condemning Russian aggression against Ukraine, the UN General Assembly called for an immediate peaceful resolution of the conflict between Russia and Ukraine and emphasized that parties to the conflict must respect human rights and international humanitarian law. We share this position. ... It is wrong to take the side of any of the warring armies, it is necessary to stand on the side of peace

and justice. Self-defense can and should be carried out by non-violent and unarmed methods.

This statement resulted in Sheliazhenko being placed under house arrest from August 15 to October 11, 2023, under the absurd charge of "justification of Russian aggression."[22]

It should be noted that there are ambiguities regarding Sheliazhenko's Ukrainian Pacifist Movement, which seems to consist of only three people. "But there are real problems in Ukraine in regards to repression related to the war," according to Hanna Perekohoda, "that are much less known to international public." She specifies: "The most problematic and shocking ones are related to 'collaboration'. People who tried to survive and to help their neighbors under the Russian occupation are accused of collaboration and put in prison. ... I think these are the examples of repression that deserve to be known and denounced."[23]

5

Views of Russian and Ukrainian socialists

There are additional matters to consider, and some to revisit, from the standpoint of Russian and Ukrainian socialists.

One matter involves how comrades understand the causes of the conflict. A second matter involves perceptions of the impact of the Russian invasion. A third involves the question of Ukrainian self-determination and of where Ukrainian arms are coming from. We will take up this third matter again in the next (and final) sections of this document. But here we will simply allow Russian and Ukrainian comrades to speak for themselves.

In analyzing the causes of the conflict, Ukrainian socialist Hanna Perekhoda goes back to the historical origins of Russia itself. "Russia did not have an empire, it was an empire" is an old expression she cites, indicating that Russia was composed of a series of conquests in which the conquered areas (or colonies) "were neither geographically nor politically separated from the imperial core." This meant that "borders, both physical and symbolic, were therefore blurred" –and Ukraine, for example, was seen as an integral and essential component of Russia. At the same time, "both the tsarist and Soviet authorities, after their Stalinist turn suppressed any manifestation of a separate Ukrainian political identity."[24] This naturally spilled over into tendencies to suppress distinctively Ukrainian language and culture.

Perekhoda goes on to suggest that developments in an independent Ukraine pose a destabilizing threat to the Putin regime's control of Russian society. To the extent that Ukraine is more free, more democratic, and more prosperous than Russia, this threatens to "awaken some dangerous ideas among Russians themselves, who are ... tired of the autocratic regime and of the extreme inequality in Russia."[25]

Russian poet Kirill Medvedev agrees: "In 2021, Putin's rating reached the lowest level it had during his entire time in power." He sees the "act of imperialist aggression by the Putin regime against Ukraine" as an effort "to strengthen his regime in the run-up to the 2024 presidential election in order to be re-elected or to be able to appoint a reliable successor."[26]

This dovetails with the discussion of the conflict's causes by Russian socialist Boris Kagarlitsky. He identifies two reasons for the war, "the first one basically global and long-term," involving the economic crises of world capitalism – particularly "the Great Recession" of 2007-8 – which "revealed the tremendous weakness of the Russian economy," detrimental to the well-being of the majority of Russians but from which the Russian oligarchs were able to benefit. Second, "people see that and see that the material situation of the great majority is getting dramatically worse, that real income is declining and prices are rising, that they are having problems getting decent jobs. All this generates tremendous discontent."[27]

Another Russian socialist, Ilya Budraitskis, emphasizes this aspect of the war – the need of the regime "to strengthen its power over its own population," making it "not just a war against Ukraine. It's a war of the Russian regime against its own society." Budraitskis elaborates:

> Since the start of the war, Putin has crushed all opposition in Russia and driven it underground and abroad. He's been successful in creating an atmosphere of fear and obedience. But only 20 percent of the population support the war enthusiastically, while about 20 percent oppose the war. The latter is, of course, repressed. Most of the rest of the society is passive and depoliticized, tolerating the status quo. Nevertheless, as Prigozhin's attempted coup proved, Putin's regime is fragile. Any serious defeat in the war could destabilize his rule and open space for social change within Russia.[28]

Ukrainian socialists vividly describe the devastating impact of the Russian invasion on their country and their people. "The Ukrainian trade union movement united about six million workers," notes labor activist Nataliya Levytska, "but now, due to the war, this number has decreased because Russia has destroyed enterprises and infrastructure, resulting in the loss of workplaces." She adds: "Russia has also destroyed residential buildings and hospitals and imposed a reign of terror in the occupied territories, forcing people to flee and become refugees."[29]

Social Movement activist Vladyslav Starodubtsev bitterly elaborates on conditions in the areas under Russian occupation:

> The situation in the occupied regions is one of occupation — it is a fascist occupation. This means repression, mass killings, holding the families of political activists hostage, repression against the LGBTIQ+ community. It is a terror state where anyone who carries out political activity is brutally

repressed. A lot of trade unions have been destroyed or forced to accept new labour contracts that are much worse than Ukrainian labour contracts, and all strikes are banned. A lot of ordinary people just went missing: they left home and never returned. There is also a lot of open looting and rapes carried out by Russian forces. The conditions are very dire.

In the occupied territories, Russian authorities have been pushing radical policies of assimilation. They have practically banned the use of the Ukrainian language and enforced the Russian language everywhere, including in schools and public administration. From September 1 [2022], when the school semester starts, the Ukrainian language will no longer be taught at any school in the occupied regions: no studying Ukrainian, no Ukrainian literature, not even within the subject of foreign literature. Russian authorities are inviting people, such as teachers and political commissars, from Russia to come to the occupied regions and

> take over positions in the education system and public administration.[30]

"Russia's imperial ambitions were reinvigorated with the fall of the Soviet Union," comments Yuliya Yurchenko. "We can see this in Putin's speeches where he refers to Ukraine as little more than a province of Russia – one without its own political subjectivity, its own culture, its own language." Boris Kagarlitsky notes that "Russian propaganda continuously states that Ukraine shouldn't exist, that Ukrainian territory is actually Russian territory that has been conquered by Ukrainians. It says Russia is going to liberate these territories from the population that lives there; that they are not the right population for that territory." He adds: "All sorts of racist, fascist statements are made on state channels. It's an absolutely incredible flood of aggression, xenophobia and hatred." Another Russian socialist, Ilya Matveev, comments: "The Russian government has never indicated that it is ready to stop this war. In fact, there are indications that it still holds on to its maximalist goal of conquering all of Ukraine, including Kyiv. I don't see any evidence that they have abandoned those goals. In that sense, a ceasefire would just play into Russian hands and prolong the war."[31]

There seems to be general agreement among the Ukrainian and Russian socialists whose perceptions we are considering that the very survival of the Ukraine has been at stake in this conflict. "Russia's invasion has created a major threat to the existence of Ukraine as an independent state," according to Vitaly Dudin. "Without doubt, we can say that the current war is the most devastating war we have seen [in Ukraine] since World War II. Putin's government has a lot of resources, but Ukrainian people are willing and ready to resist." This struggle for survival is naturally linked to the question of armaments. "The future of demilitarization lies in stopping Russia's war machine now," Dudin asserts. "Issues of security should be of strong concern. Any demilitarisation that ignores the security of the people, their right to defend themselves, and justifies blocking resistance against imperialist aggression is morally wrong."[32]

Perekhoda emphasizes that "for Ukraine, this is a war of self-defense. And I think it's very important to make a difference between, you know, the use of violence with the aim of aggression and the use of violence with the aim to protect your own existence." This means "the question of weapons is essential to us because it's the question of our survival as a society and of our political, economic sovereignty." Medvedev of the Russian Socialist Movement suggests that the Putin regime's denunciation of Ukraine for getting weapons from the United States and Western Europe seems questionable since "Russia has also been buying weapons from the West for years." More than this, notes this Russian socialist, "Ukraine, as a country subject to intervention, has every right to receive military aid from anyone — just like the Kurds, and just like Vietnam in the 1960s and 1970s."[33]

6

Lessons from history on self-determination

Not all Marxist-oriented socialists are necessarily inclined to accept the analysis of Putin presented here.[34] Nor is the analysis of the Russia-Ukrainian conflict presented here embraced by all who identify as revolutionary Marxists. In fact, considerable time and space and energy have been devoted to fierce denunciations and counter-denunciations among such groups on this question. Much of this does not strike me as having been fruitful. My hope is that we can move forward in a manner that helps to unite rather than fragment our movement, through frank and comradely discussion.

The approach advanced here, it should be admitted, is not an original contribution. It is grounded in the orientation that V.I. Lenin outlined in such works as *The Right of Nations to Self Determination* (1914) and "The Revolutionary Proletariat Socialist Revolution and the Right of Nations to Self-Determination" (1915). As the First World War erupted, some excellent revolutionaries – including Rosa Luxemburg and some comrades in the Bolshevik party – argued that all forms of nationalism are incompatible with working-class internationalism. Lenin sharply took issue with this conclusion. There are different forms of nationalism – some worthy of support, others worthy of denunciation. A distinction must be made between the nationalism (to be opposed) of the imperialist nations and the nationalism (to be supported) of those countries oppressed by imperialism. As he put it in *Socialism and War* (1915), revolutionaries must "unequivocally demand that the socialists of the oppressing countries (of the so-called 'great' nations in particular) should recognize and

WELL YOU MOBILE MASSAGE

"Harmony in body, Mind and soul promotes a true state of health, peace and happiness"

Choose 60/90/120 min of treatment
Price £65/85/115

Massage

Relaxing massage
Deep Tissue massage
Lymphatic Drainage and after operation care
Pregnancy massage

doTERRA Aroma Touch

AromaTouch massage with power of doTERRA essential oils to create and promote homeostasis in Your body

treatment 45 min £70 or add on to any other treatment.
Ask for details

Face & Body

Japanese Facial Massage
treatment 90 min £90

Madotherapy - Wood Therapy
(body contouring, anticellulite, lymph circulation)

CALL 07729908400

defend the right of the oppressed nations to self-determination."[35]

After the overthrow of the tsar in early 1917, Lenin was sharply critical of the Russian moderates of the Provisional Government for not recognizing Ukraine's right to independence. "Russia's revolutionary democrats, if they want to be truly revolutionary and truly democratic," Lenin insisted, "must regain for themselves, for the workers and peasants of Russia, the brotherly trust of the Ukrainian workers and peasants. This cannot be done without full recognition of the Ukraine's rights, including the *right* to free secession." He wryly commented that Russian "friendship" could not be imposed on Ukrainians but could only be won by treating Ukrainians as equals and acknowledging their right to secede from Russia if they chose.[36]

When the Provisional Government was removed by the October 1917 revolution, the socialist government that Lenin now headed affirmed, more than once, "that the right to self-determination belongs to all nations oppressed by tsarism and the Great Russian bourgeoisie, up to and including the right of these nations to secede from Russia." Flowing from this, the Bolshevik regime declared that "we ... recognise the People's Ukrainian Republic, and its right to secede from Russia or enter into a treaty with the Russian Republic on federal or similar relations between them." Lenin insisted on recognition "at once, unconditionally and without reservations [of] everything that pertains to the Ukrainian people's national rights and national independence."[37]

Serious historians have traced the complexities of what happened next. Despite Lenin's position on Ukrainian self-determination, comments Hanna Perekhoda, on the ground "the local Bolsheviks were overwhelmed by events for which they were ill-prepared." In the swirl of the Russian civil war (in which the Ukraine was a central battleground), anti-Bolshevik nationalists seized control of the independence movement. Fighting for their lives, the Bolsheviks on the scene fumbled badly more than once in relation to the question of self-determination, riding roughshod over the formal Bolshevik commitments and driving many Ukrainians into open conflict with the new revolutionary regime. This greatly benefitted the counter-revolutionary White armies of General Anton Denikin.[38]

Throughout 1919, the Red Army battled to reverse this deteriorating situation. Late in the year its commander, Leon Trotsky, issued a proclamation to his troops, re-emphasizing Lenin's earlier position:

> Ukraine is the land of the Ukrainian workers and working peasants. They alone have the right to rule in Ukraine, to govern it and to build a new life in it. ... Keep this firmly in mind: your task is not to conquer Ukraine but to liberate it. When Denikin's bands have finally been smashed, the working people of the liberated Ukraine will themselves decide on what terms they are to live with Soviet Russia. We are all sure, and we know, that the working people of Ukraine will declare for the closest fraternal union with us. ... Long live the free and independent Soviet Ukraine![39]

The Bolsheviks (now renamed Communists) shifted to this orientation. Lenin authored a resolution making it "incumbent on all party members to use every means to help remove all barriers in the way of the free development of the Ukrainian language and culture ... suppressed for centuries by Russian Tsarism and the exploiting classes." Historian Ronald Suny observes: "By the end of that civil war, Ukraine was more or less integrated into the Soviet Union. In the constitution of that early Soviet Union, Ukraine and the other Union republics were given the right to secede without any preconditions."[40]

"Ukraine was a devastated country at the end of the civil war," notes Mario Kessler. "The years 1921 and 1922 were marked by a catastrophic famine." Yet Leninist policy continued even as conditions of civil war and famine were left behind. "The situation began to improve following the constitution the Union of Soviet Socialist Republics (USSR), which Ukraine joined as a founding member in late 1922: the New Economic Policy (NEP) facilitated an economic recovery, the Ukrainian language and culture were promoted, and after the elimination of antisemitic legislation, Jewish intellectual culture experienced an unprecedented boom."[41]

All of this was reversed, however, after the 1920s victory of Stalin's faction over his opponents, in the Russian Communist Party. Moving against "nationalist deviations," in a brutal reversal of Bolshevik policy, Stalin's policies brought new horrors. In the Ukraine, "forced collectivization of agriculture, economically induced famine, and brutal political persecution," Kessler recounts, "including starvation of entire territories, the Holodomor (the Ukrainian term for 'killing by starvation') cost the lives of at least 4 million people."[42]

From exile in 1939, Trotsky protested against Stalin's policies. The Soviet bureaucratic dictatorship, he commented, had "strangled and plundered the people within Great Russia," but "in the Ukraine matters were further complicated by the massacre of national hopes. Nowhere did restrictions, purges, repressions and in general all forms of bureaucratic hooliganism assume such murderous sweep as they did in the Ukraine in the struggle against the powerful, deeply rooted longings of the Ukrainian masses for greater freedom and independence."[43]

Of course, much has changed over the past century, but what happened yesterday can still teach us something today. Those who have opposing orientations in our own time will secure different lessons from history. Putin's position is that the policies of Lenin and the Bolsheviks (Trotsky included) seriously undermined Russian national interests, while Stalin's policies represented an important correction. Those who are committed to genuine democracy and revolutionary socialism, however, may have more to learn from Lenin and his comrades.[44]

7

Where the weapons come from

If one seriously acknowledges the right of an oppressed nation to self-determination, and therefore to resist invasion from an oppressor nation, then it must be recognized that the oppressed nation has a right to secure weapons for this purpose.

A major point of contention for those opposing armed resistance of Ukrainians against the Russian invasion, however, is that the weapons necessary for such armed resistance are being supplied by Western imperialist powers, especially the United States.

For some, this means that the Ukrainians are

doing the bidding of U.S. imperialism, which is seen as the greatest threat to peace and freedom on our planet. Employing the logic that "the enemy of our enemy is our friend," some conclude that the Putin regime should be supported by all progressives who favor peace and freedom. There are others who do not believe that, but who still oppose the arming of the Ukrainian resistance by Western imperialism.

Anti-imperialists have not always denounced accepting arms from Western imperialist countries. During the Spanish Civil War of 1936-39, the newly formed Spanish Republic was subjected to a military onslaught by a right-wing coalition supported (and largely armed) by fascist Italy and Nazi Germany. The Republic was defended by a coalition of liberals, socialists, communists (of both Stalinist and anti-Stalinist persuasion), and anarchists – a coalition that was poorly armed. The so-called "Western democracies" – consisting of imperialist countries that included the United States, Britain, and France – imposed an arms embargo on Spain. Since this would give a considerable advantage to the right-wing and fascist forces (receiving plenty of arms from Germany and Italy), the embargo was fiercely denounced by left-wing activists throughout the world. There was widespread agitation for the Western (imperialist) democracies to aid the Spanish Republic.[45]

In the same period, the military forces of Imperial Japan were invading the Chinese Republic, headed by a nationalist dictatorship of Chiang Kai-Shek, which in the late 1930s was compelled to form a United Front with Chinese Communists to oppose the Japanese onslaught. Here too, a campaign was waged (including by left-wing activists throughout the world) to secure military aid from the Western imperialist rivals of Imperial Japan.[46]

It is worth pausing for a moment regarding the Chinese example, since Chiang Kai-shek's regime certainly did not have the progressive-democratic qualities which many saw in the Spanish Republic. "We need have no illusions about Chiang Kai-shek, his party, or the whole ruling class of China," Trotsky argued at the time. "Chiang Kai-shek is the executioner of the Chinese workers and peasants," Trotsky acknowledged. "But today he is forced, despite himself, to struggle against

Japan for the remainder of the independence of China. Tomorrow he may again betray. ... But today he is struggling." Trotsky emphasized what he saw as the key point: "If Japan is an imperialist country and if China is the victim of imperialism, we favor China. Japanese patriotism is the hideous mask of worldwide robbery. Chinese patriotism is legitimate and progressive."[47] As it turned out, of course, U.S. policymakers who ultimately supplied Chiang Kai-shek were maneuvering to advance U.S. imperial interests in China. But this neither obviates the validity of Trotsky's point nor was capable of preventing the later advance of the Chinese Revolution.

There are innumerable examples that can be found of revolutionaries, freedom fighters, and leaders of resistance struggles against imperialism securing weapons by any means necessary, even from sources representing the opposite of what one is fighting for. One of the most outstanding examples can be found in the American Revolution of 1775-83, in which money, arms, and direct military support from the French monarchy helped anti-colonial revolutionaries of North America to

MAKING SENSE OF RUSSIA'S INVASION OF UKRAINE

break free from the British monarchy.[48] Some argue that imperialist powers providing such assistance are only interested in advancing their own imperial interests, always seeking to manipulate the situation for their own advantage. Absolutely – that is what imperialists always do.

It is also true (for example, in the case of the American Revolution) that revolutionaries are also seeking to manipulate the situation (including the aid received) for the advantage of their revolutionary cause. It would have been a mistake for American revolutionaries, in exchange for French assistance, to violate revolutionary principles by integrating themselves into the French Empire – just as it would be a mistake, in my opinion, for revolutionaries of today to integrate themselves into NATO. But it is not a mistake, in a life and death struggle, for freedom fighters to accept weapons from either the French monarchy of 1778 or from nations belonging to NATO in 2023. And it makes no sense to withhold support because revolutionaries are not getting weapons exclusively from angels. If the cause of revolutionaries and freedom fighters is just, they will be inclined to struggle for victory by any means necessary.

Notes

1. The primary threat, I think, involves Ukraine's pulling away from Russia, rather than the presence of NATO.

2. Classic works illustrating this imperialist reality include: Scott Nearing and Joseph Freeman, *Dollar Diplomacy, A Study in American Imperialism* (New York: Monthly Review Press, 1966); William Appleman Williams, *The Tragedy of American Diplomacy*, 50th Anniversary Edition (New York: W. W. Norton, 2009); Harry Magdoff, *Imperialism: from the*

Colonial Age to the Present (New York: Monthly Review Press, 1978); William Blum, *Killing Hope: US Military and CIA Interventions since World War II*, Updated Edition (London: Bloomsbury Academic, 2022). Among those tracing this back to the 1790s are: Kenneth Bowling, "American Empire and the Nation's Founding," C-SPAN, September 10, 2016, https://www.c-span.org/video/?413808-1/american-empire-nations-founding; Richard N. Van Alstyne, *The Rising American Empire*, Second Edition (New York: W. W. Norton, 1974); William Appleman Williams, *Empire as a Way of Life* (New York: Oxford University Press, 1982).

3. See an informative debate on the nature of present-day Russian imperialism: Claudio Katz, "Is Russia an Imperialist Power?" in *Links: International Journal of Socialist Renewal* (1) https://links.org.au/russia-imperialist-power-part-i-non-hegemonic-

gestation, (2) https://links.org.au/russia-imperialist-power-part-ii-lenins-legacy, (3) https://links.org.au/russia-imperialist-power-part-iii-continuities-reconstructions-and-ruptures, (4) https://links.org.au/russia-imperialist-power-part-iv-benevolent-glances; Michael Pröbsting (interviewed by Federico Fuentes), "Imperialism, Great Power Rivalry, and Revolutionary Strategy in the Twenty-First Century," *Links: International Journal of Socialist Renewal*, 1 September 2023, https://links.org.au/imperialism-great-power-rivalry-and-revolutionary-strategy-twenty-first-century; John Smith (interviewed by Federico Fuentes), "Twenty-first Century Imperialism, Multi-Polarity, and Capitalism's 'Final Crisis,'" *Links: International Journal of Socialist Renewal*, 1 August 2023, https://links.org.au/twenty-first-century-imperialism-multipolarity-and-capitalisms-final-crisis.

4. This and the following Mersheimer quotes are taken from Isaac Chotiner, "Why John Mearsheimer Blames the U.S. for the Crisis in Ukraine" (interview), *New Yorker*, March 1, 2022, https://www.newyorker.com/news/q-and-a/why-john-mearsheimer-blames-the-us-for-the-crisis-in-ukraine. Additional information on the realities Mersheimer alludes to can be found in Ronald G. Suny, "Ukraine War Follows Two Decades of Warnings That NATO Expansion into Eastern Europe Could Provoke Russia," *The Conversation*, Feb. 22, 2022, https://theconversation.com/ukraine-war-follows-decades-of-warnings-that-nato-expansion-into-eastern-europe-could-provoke-russia-177999.

5. Medea Benjamin and Nicholas J.S. Davies, *War in Ukraine: Making Sense of a Senseless Conflict* (New York: OR Books, 2022), 149. Also worth consulting is a critical review of this book by David Finkel, "Making Sense of a Senseless Conflict in

Ukraine?" *Counterpunch*, Dec. 23, 2022, https://www.counterpunch.org/2022/12/23/making-sense-of-a-senseless-conflict/.

6. Matthew Gibson, "The Essence of Putin's Managed Democracy" (Summary), Carnegie Endowment for International Peace, October 8, 2005, https://carnegieendowment.org/2005/10/18/essence-of-putin-s-managed-democracy-event-819; Martin Russell, "Russia: Political Parties in a 'Managed Democracy,'" European Parliament, Membership Research Service, Dec. 2014; Maxim Trudolyubov, "Putin's Managed Democracy Falters," Russia File, Kennan Institute, Sept. 27, 2018, https://www.wilsoncenter.org/blog-post/putins-managed-democracy-falters.

7. Michel Eltchanoff, *Inside the Mind of Vladimir Putin* (London: Hurst & Co., 2018); Andrei Kolesnikov, "The End of the Russian Idea: What It Will Take to Break Putinism's Grip," *Foreign Affairs*, Septem-

ber/October 2023; Santiago Zabala, Claudio Gallo, "Putin's Philosophers: Who Inspired Him to Invade Ukraine?" *Aljazeera*, 30 March 2022 https://www.aljazeera.com/opinions/2022/3/30/putins-philosophers?traffic_source=KeepReading.

8. A useful documentary dramatically bringing this all together is Nick Schifrin/Zach Fannin, "Inside Putin's Russia," PBS News Hour, July 21, 2017, https://www.youtube.com/watch?v=_AkAZIk73F0.

On the Russian Orthodox Church, see Andrei Soldatov and Irina Borogan, "Putin's Useful Priests: The Russian Orthodox Church and the Kremlin's Hidden Influence Campaign in the West," *Foreign Affairs*, September/October 2023.

On Cossacks, see Jolanta Darczewska, *Putin's Cossacks: Folklore, Business or Politics?* Point of View, Number 68 (Warsaw: Ośrodek Studiów Wschodnich im. Marka karpia/Centre for Eastern Studies, December 2017) www.osw.waw.pl/sites/default/

files/pw_68_putin_cossacks_net_0.pdf.

It is well worth considering multiple presentations by Putin regarding the Ukraine. For a short, defensive explanation, see Vladimir Putin, "On conducting a special military operation, Feb. 24, 2022, https://en.wikipedia.org/wiki/On_conducting_a_special_military_operation. For a more elaborate "Great Russia" explanation, see Vladimir Putin, "Statement on Ukraine," Feb. 21, 2022, https://www.c-span.org/video/?518097-2/russian-president-putin-statement-ukraine. He offers a significant historical survey in Vladimir Putin, "On the Historical Unity of Russians and Ukrainians," Official Internet Resources of the President of Russia, July 12, 2021, http://en.kremlin.ru/events/president/news/66181.

9. Ilya Budraitskis and Hanna Perekhoda (interview with Ashley Smith), "Resisting Russian Imperialism: Two Socialists – a Ukrainian and a Russian – on Ukraine's

Struggle for Self-Determination," *The Nation*, Sept. 7, 2023, https://www.thenation.com/article/archive/resisting-russian-imperialism-2-socialists-a-ukrainian-and-a-russian-on-ukraines-struggle-for-self-determination/.

10. Brief videos on what happened in Russia include: "Russian Capitalism After Communism," History, Feb. 22, 2019, https://www.youtube.com/watch?v=ui8p3MEWW78; "The Modern Economy of Russia," Economics Explained (Australia), Dec. 15, 2019, https://www.youtube.com/watch?v=6wBvG533K8A; and Vladimir Buzgalin (interviewed by Paul Jay), "Putin and Navalny Both Represent Big Russian Capital," Feb. 21, 2021, https://theanalysis.news/putin-and-navalny-both-represent-big-russian-capital-alexander-buzgalin/.https://theanalysis.news/putin-and-navalny-both-represent-big-russian-capital-alexander-buzgalin/

Substantial Marxist analyses on Russia can be found in: Simon Pirani, *Change in Putin's Russia: Power, Money and People* (London: Pluto Press, 2010), and Ruslan Dzarasov, *The Conundrum of Russian Capitalism: The Post-Soviet Economy in the World System* (London: Pluto Press, 2013). For somewhat similar analyses on Ukraine see: Yuliya Yurchenko, *Ukraine and the Empire of Capital: From Marketisation to Armed Conflict* (London: Pluto Press, 2018), and Renfrey Clarke, *The Catastrophe of Ukrainian Capitalism: How Privatisation Dispossessed and Impoverished the Ukrainian People* (Australia: Resistance Books, 2022).

The transition from the Union of Soviet Socialist Republics to the Russian regime of Vladimir Putin is outlined in a very interesting set of interviews with a Marxist who lived through it. See Vladimir Buzgalin (interviewed by Paul Jay), "Soviet Union and post-Soviet Russia," The Real News Network/The Analysis, July 2018:

- Growing Up in the USSR, https://therealnews.com/growing-up-in-the-ussr-rai-with-a-buzgalin-1-12
- Success and Mutation in the Soviet Union, https://theanalysis.news/success-and-mutation-in-the-soviet-union-rai-with-aleksandr-buzgalin/
- Communism and Consumerism, https://theanalysis.news/communism-and-consumerism-rai-with-aleksandr-buzgalin-3-12/
- Turning Power into Money, https://theanalysis.news/turning-power-into-money-the-end-of-the-soviet-union-rai-with-aleksandr-buzgalin-4-12/
- Collapse of Soviet Union, https://theanalysis.news/i-returned-from-vacation-to-find-the-soviet-union-had-collapsed-rai-with-aleksandr-buzgalin-5-12/
- New Russia: Chaos and Plunder, https://theanalysis.news/shock-

- without-the-therapy-a-new-russia-is-born-in-chaos-and-plunder-rai-with-aleksandr-buzgalin-6-12/
- Putin is Anointed, https://theanalysis.news/putin-is-anointed-king-but-big-capital-has-the-real-power-rai-with-aleksandr-buzgalin-7-12/
- Is Putin's Rule a Dictatorship? https://theanalysis.news/is-putins-rule-a-dictatorship-rai-with-aleksandr-buzgalin/
- Putin Popular, Russian People Poor, https://theanalysis.news/why-is-putin-so-popular-when-people-are-so-poor-rai-with-aleksandr-buzgalin-9-12/
- Why Does the West Hate Putin? https://theanalysis.news/why-does-the-west-hate-putin-rai-with-aleksandr-buzgalin-10-12/
- Climate Crisis and Economics, https://theanalysis.news/many-russians-think-climate-change-is-propaganda-to-weaken-their-

- economy-rai-with-aleksandr-buzgalin-11-12/
  - Artificial Intelligence and Future of Socialism, https://theanalysis.news/artificial-intelligence-and-the-future-of-socialism-rai-with-aleksandr-buzgalin-12-12/

11. Serhii Plokhy, *The Russo-Ukrainian War: The Return of History* (New York: W.W. Norton, 2023), 36, 45.

12. Clarke, 18.

13. Pirani, 62.

14. Yurchenko, 1.

15. Yurchenko, xiii-xiv.

16. A coherent account of the war is presented on pages 135-242 of Plokhy's *The Russo-Ukrainian War*, the book's first half covering the historical background and developments leading up to the war.

Plokhy's scholarly work is inflected with a liberal-oriented nationalism that is deeply sympathetic to his native Ukraine.

17. Federico Fuentes, ed., *Ukraine Resists! Left Voices on Putin's War, NATO the Future of Ukraine* (Australia: Resistance Books, 2023), 29. For a useful survey of the Ukrainian left, see Catherine Samary, "A Ukrainian Left Under Construction on Several Fronts," *Links: International Journal of Socialist Renewal*, 21 October 2022, https://links.org.au/ukrainian-left-under-construction-several-fronts-national-conference-sotsialnyi-rukhsocial-movement. Additional information is provided in Vladyslav Starodubtsev, "Resistance and Solidarity. The Left Volunteer Movement in the Russo-Ukrainian War," *Links: International Journal of Socialist Renewal*, 18 November 2022, https://links.org.au/resistance-and-solidarity-left-volunteer-movement-russo-ukrainian-war. For a revealing video of

left-wing combatants and activists in the Ukrainian resistance, see Enguerran Carrier, "Ukraine: Revolutionaries at War," August 2022, https://www.youtube.com/watch?v=NW2X4Naw_YY

18. Fuentes, 25, 36.

19. Budraitskis and Perekhoda (*Nation* interview).

20. Information on Nazis in Ukraine can be found in "Nazis in Ukraine," Full Measure with Sharyl Attkisson, Jan. 16, 2023, https://www.youtube.com/watch?v=m4ngne9AGWM and Josh Cohen, "Ukraine's Neo-Nazi Problem," Reuter's, March 19, 2018, https://www.reuters.com/article/us-cohen-ukraine-commentary/commentary-ukraines-neo-nazi-problem-idUSKBN1GV2TY. On Russia, See "Putin's Secret Neo-Nazi Armies: Decade of Hate," Vice, Aug. 22, 2022; https://www.youtube.com/

watch?v=XQc6mJ7u8gQ. On the danger in both countries, see Odette Youseff, "The Russian-Ukraine Conflict Could Strengthen Neo-Fascist Groups in Both Countries," National Public Radio, March 5m 2022, https://www.npr.org/2022/03/05/1084729572/the-russian-ukraine-conflict-could-strengthen-neo-fascist-groups-in-both-countries. Quotation from Boris Kagarlitsky in Fuentes, 66.

21. Putin quote in Eltchaninoff, *Inside the Mind of Vladimir Putin*, 15. Also revealing on this matter is "A Small Town Clings to Its Soviet Past" DW (Deutsche Welle) Documentary, 2019, https://www.youtube.com/watch?v=48DaLYiO-yk. On anti-war dissidents in Russia, see: "Putin's War at Home," PBS Frontline, Nov. 1, 2022, https://www.pbs.org/wgbh/frontline/documentary/putins-war-at-home/, Boris Kagarlistsky (interviewed by Paul Jay), "How Will the Ukraine War End?" The Analysis, Feb. 23, 2023, https://www.you-

tube.com/watch?v=Kezxsu09mrQ; Paul Jay (interviewed by Talia Baroncelli), "Russian Anti-War Activist - Boris Kagarlitsky Arrested," July 31, 2023, https://www.youtube.com/watch?v=0L1C6vUTPX0. On the growth of strong far-right elements in Russia, see: Sergey Sukhankin, "'Russia for Russians!' Ultranationalism and xenophobia in Russia: from marginality to state promoted philosophy," CIDOB Notes Internationals 128, Sept. 2015, https://www.cidob.org/en/publications/publication_series/notes_internacionals/n1_128_russia_for_russians/russia_for_russians_ultranationalism_and_xenophobia_in_russia_from_marginality_to_state_promoted_philosophy; Katharina Bluhm and Mihai Varga, "Russia's Right-Wing Reaction to the War," PONARS Eurasia, April 28, 2022,https://www.ponarseurasia.org/russias-right-wing-reactions-to-the-war/. Oleg Ignatov, "Russia's Shifting Far-Right: The 'War Party,'" *The Interpreter*, 5

April 2023, https://www.lowyinstitute.org/the-interpreter/russia-s-shifting-far-right-war-party.

22. War Resisters League International, "Ukraine: Release peace activist Yurii Sheliazhenko and drop all charges against him," 17 Aug. 2023, https://wri-irg.org/en/story/2023/ukraine-release-peace-activist-yurii-sheliazhenko-and-drop-all-charges-against-him; Marcy Winograd, "Ukrainian Pacifist Movement: An Interview with Yurii Sheliazhenko," *Counterpunch*, Jan. 19, 2023, https://www.counterpunch.org/2023/01/19/ukrainian-pacifist-movement-an-interview-with-yurii-sheliazhenko/ ; Ukrainian Pacifist Movement, "Peace Agenda for Ukraine and the World," September 21, 2022, World Beyond War, https://worldbeyondwar.org/peace-agenda-for-ukraine-and-the-world/.

23. Hanna Perekhoda, email to author, October 18, 2023. For more information,

see: https://graty.me/themes/speczpro%d1%94kt-liman-chuzhi-sered-svo%d1%97h/.

24. Fuentes, 16.

25. Ilya Budraitskis and Hanna Perekhoda (interview with Nermeen Shaikh and Amy Goodman), "Ukrainian & Russian Activists on How Putin's War Emboldens 'Authoritarian Forces' Around the World," Democracy Now, Sept. 7, 2023, https://www.democracynow.org/2023/9/7/hanna_perekhoda_ilya_budraitskis_ukraine_russia.

26. Fuentes, 82.

27. Fuentes, 63, 64.

28. Budraitskis and Perekhoda (Democracy Now interview); bloc quote from Budraitskis and Perekhoda (*Nation* interview). The coup attempt involved former Putin ally Yevgeny Prigozhin, head of the so-called

Wagner group, a Russian state-funded private military company formed in 2014, which sent over 20,000 fighters into the Russian-Ukraine conflict. See the Wikipedia entry "Yevgeny Prigozhin" –https://en.wikipedia.org/wiki/Yevgeny_Prigozhin.

29. Fuentes, 36.

30. Fuentes, 27-28.

31. Fuentes, 12, 62, 59.

32. Fuentes, 22, 25.

33. Budraitskis and Perekhoda (Democracy Now interview); Fuentes, 84, 83.

34. One particularly sad example involves Roy and Zhores Medvedev, outstanding dissident Marxists of the Soviet era who allowed themselves to be disoriented and seduced by the Putin regime, joining with their one-time adversary in the dissident movement, anti-Marxist conservative Alexander

Solzhenitsyn, in an embrace of the regime. See Barbara Martin, *Roy and Zhores Medvedev, Loyal Dissent in the Soviet Union* (Boston: Academic Studies Press, 2023), 208-19, and Robin Ashenden, "Would Solzhenitsyn Have Supported Putin's War?" *The Spectator*, 27 Nov. 2022, https://www.spectator.co.uk/article/would-solzhenitsyn-have-supported-putins-war/.

35. Marxist Internet Archive: Vladimir Ilyich Lenin, *The Right of Nations to Self-Determination*, https://www.marxists.org/archive/lenin/works/1914/self-det/ch01.htm; Vladimir Ilyich Lenin, "The Revolutionary Proletariat and the Right of Nations to Self-Determination," https://www.marxists.org/archive/lenin/works/1915/oct/16.htm; Vladimir Ilyich Lenin, *Socialism and War* (with G. Zinoviev), Chapter One, https://www.marxists.org/archive/lenin/works/1915/s-w/ch01.htm.

36. Marxist Internet Archive: Vladimir Ilyich Lenin, "The Ukraine," https://www.marxists.org/archive/lenin/works/1917/jun/28.htm.

37. Marxist Internet Archive: Vladimir Ilyich Lenin, "Manifesto to the Ukrainian People," https://www.marxists.org/archive/lenin/works/1917/dec/03.htm.

38. Hanna Perekhoda,"When the Bolsheviks Created a Soviet Republic in the Donbas," *Jacobin*, March 22, 2022, https://jacobin.com/2022/03/bolshevik-soviet-republic-donbas-ukraine-national-question-lenin-putin-ussr; Zbigniew Marcin Kowalewski, "For the Independence of Soviet Ukraine," Historical Materialism, 12 March 2022, https://www.historicalmaterialism.org/blog/for-independence-soviet-ukraine; Doug Tribou interviewing Ronald G. Suny, "From Lenin to Putin: Key turning points in Russian-Ukrainian history 1922-2022," NPR Morning Edition, Michigan Public Radio, March 4, 2022,

https://www.michiganradio.org/politics-government/2022-03-04/from-lenin-to-putin-key-turning-points-in-russian-ukrainian-history-1922-2022; Plokhy, 15-18.

39. L. Trotsky, *How the Revolution Armed*, vol. 2, (London: New Park Publications, 1979), 439; Marxist Internet Archive, "Order No. 174," https://www.marxists.org/archive/trotsky/1919/military/ch108.htm.

40. Marxist Internet Archive: Vladimir Ilyich Lenin, "On Soviet Rule in the Ukraine," https://www.marxists.org/archive/lenin/works/1919/nov/x01.htm; Suny in Doug Tribou interview.

41. Mario Kessler, "The Forgotten History of Ukrainian Independence," Rosa Luxemburg Stiftung, March 21, 2022, https://www.rosalux.de/en/news/id/46176.

42. Kessler; Plokhy, 18-19. Also see Vadim Rogovin, "The Restoration of the Imperial Idea in Stalin's USSR," *Links: International Journal of Socialist Renewal*, 7 September 2023, https://links.org.au/restoration-imperial-idea-stalins-ussr.

43. Kowalewski; Marxist Internet Archive: Leon Trotsky, "The Problem of the Ukraine" (1939), https://www.marxists.org/archive/trotsky/1939/04/ukraine.html.

44. For a useful and even more elaborate discussion of certain matters deal with here, see Jerry Harris, "Marxism and Ukraine's Struggle for Independence and Self-Determination," *Links: International Journal of Socialist Renewal*, September 2023, https://links.org.au/marxism-and-ukraines-struggle-independence-and-self-determination.

45. Among the reliable accounts of the Spanish Civil War is Pierre Broué and Émile

Témime, *The Revolution and Civil War in Spain 1934-1939* (Chicago: Haymarket Books, 2008). The devastating impact of the arms embargo for the Spanish Republic is documented in Gerald Howson, *Arms for Spain: The Untold Story of the Spanish Civil War* (New York: St. Martin's Press, 1999).

46. See Rana Mitter's appropriately titled *Forgotten Ally: China's World War II 1937-1945* (New York: Houghton Mifflin Harcourt, 2013)

47. Marxist Internet Archive: Leon Trotsky, "On the Sino-Japanese War" (Sept. 1937), https://www.marxists.org/archive/trotsky/1937/10/sino.htm.

48. Paul Le Blanc, "Was George Washington a French Agent?" *Socialist Worker*, June 27, 2017, https://socialistworker.org/2017/06/27/was-george-washington-a-french-agent

Chronology of events

Dec. 1, 1991: Ukraine becomes independent by overwhelming popular vote, following collapse of the Union of Soviet Socialist Republics (USSR).

Dec. 5, 1994: The Budapest Memorandum is signed by governments of Ukraine, Russia, the United States and United Kingdom, honoring Ukraine's sovereignty and its rights to its territory, following Ukraine's agreement to transfer all nuclear weapons to the Russian Federation.

November – December 2004: Orange Revolution overturns election results. Presidential election between Western-oriented candidate

Viktor Yushchenko and Russian-oriented Viktor Yanukovych, who was supported by Russia, marred by manipulations resulting in Yanukovych victory, widely seen as fraudulent. Mass protests (in which protestors wore orange, Yushchenko's campaign color) force a re-vote, resulting in Yushchenko victory.

April 3, 2008: Russia fights Ukrainian NATO membership. NATO summit meeting considers extending membership to Ukraine. Russian President Vladimir Putin expresses sharp opposition, causing NATO not to offer membership to Ukraine.

January 2010: Orange Revolution "hero" voted out. Widespread corruption and policies bringing economic hardship to many cause Yushchenko to lose the presidential election to pro-Russian rival Yanukovych, who now promised affiliation with the European Union (EU) and economic well-being.

November 2013 to February 2014: Euromaidan protests. President Yanukovych – whose policies fail to uproot corruption – changes political direction, orienting Ukraine toward Russia and implementing authoritarian political measures. Widespread protests erupt throughout the country, centering on Maidan Square in the capital, Kyiv. After the failure of violent repression, Yanukovych flees to Russia and a new leadership commits to orienting toward the EU.

February 2014 to March 2014: Russia takes Crimea. Russian-backed separatists seize control of Crimea, a Ukrainian peninsula with a predominantly ethnic Russian population, in the aftermath of the Euromaidan protests. At request of the separatists, Russian military occupies Crimea, which is then annexed to the Russian Federation. This is condemned by the United Nations and the European Union.

April 2014: Pro-Russian separatists seize government buildings in Donbas region. Proclaiming independence from Ukraine, separatists establish Donetsk People's Republic and the Luhansk People's Republic, with military support from Russia, despite Ukrainian attempts to retake separatist-held areas.

April 21, 2019: Volodymyr Zelenskyy elected President of Ukraine. Volodymyr Zelenskyy overwhelmingly wins presidential election, and his party wins a majority in Parliament – promising an end to widespread corruption and an end to the war in eastern Ukraine.

December 2021: Putin demands security guarantees. Putin publishes an article claiming that Russians and Ukrainians are "one people," and by December, tens of thousands of Russian troops are massed on Ukraine's borders. Putin's demand that Ukraine never be admitted to NATO is rejected by the Biden administration.

Feb. 21, 2022: Russia recognizes breakaway Ukrainian regions as sovereign. Formally recognizing the Donestk People's Republic and Luhansk People's Republic as independent states, Putin sends troops there to "keep the peace."

Feb. 24, 2022: Russia launches full-scale invasion of Ukraine.

10

Ukrainian and solidarity organisations

Social Movement / Соціальний рух
https://www.facebook.com/social.ruh

Commons, journal of social criticism / Спільне
https://commons.com.ua/en

Feminist Workshop / Феміністична майстерня
https://femwork.org/pro-nas

SD Platform / СД Платформа
https://sdplatform.org.ua/main/en

Federation of Trade Unions of Ukraine / Федерація профспілок України
https://www.fpsu.org.ua

Confederation of Free Trade Unions of Ukraine / Конфедерація вільних профспілок України
https://kvpu.org.ua/en

European Network for Solidarity with Ukraine
https://www.facebook.com/EuropeUkraine-Solidarity

Ukraine Solidarity Campaign (Britain)
https://ukrainesolidaritycampaign.org

Ukraine Information Group
https://ukraine-solidarity.org

Ukraine Solidarity Campaign Scotland
https://www.facebook.com/USCScotland

Irish Left With Ukraine
https://www.facebook.com/groups/irishleft-withukraine

Ukraine Solidarity Network US
https://www.facebook.com/UkraineSolidarityUS

Ukraine Socialist Solidarity Campaign (US)
https://www.facebook.com/groups/307530784861174

WHAT IS A*CR

Anti*Capitalist Resistance is an organisation of revolutionary socialists. We believe red-green revolution is necessary to meet the compound crisis of humanity and the planet.

We are internationalists, ecosocialists, and anti-capitalist revolutionaries. We oppose imperialism, nationalism, and militarism, and all forms of discrimination, oppression, and bigotry. We support the self-organisation of women, Black people, disabled people, and LGBTQI+ people. We support all oppressed people fighting imperialism and forms of apartheid, and struggling for self-determination, including the people of Palestine.

We favour mass resistance to neoliberal capitalism. We work inside existing mass organisations, but we believe grassroots struggle to be the core of effective resistance, and that the emancipation of the working class and the oppressed will be the act of the working class and the oppressed ourselves.

We reject forms of left organisation that focus exclusively on electoralism and social-democratic reforms. We also oppose top-down 'democratic centralist' models. We favour a pluralist organisation that can learn from struggles at home and across the world.

We aim to build a united organisation, rooted in the struggles of the working class and the oppressed, and committed to debate, initiative, and self-activity. We are for social transformation, based on mass participatory democracy.

info@anticapitalistresistance.org
www.anticapitalistresistance.org

ABOUT RESISTANCE BOOKS

Resistance Books is a radical publisher of internationalist and ecosocialist books. We publish books in collaboration with Anti*Capitalist Resistance (www.anticapitalistresistance.org), the International Institute for Research and Education in Amsterdam (www.iire.org) and the Fourth International (www.fourth.international/en). For further information, including a full list of titles available and how to order them, go to the Resistance Books website.

info@resistancebooks.org
www.resistancebooks.org

OTHER POCKET BOOKS

Making Sense of Russia's Invasion of Ukraine
Paul Le Blanc.

Capitalist China and Socialist Revolution
Simon Hannah.

Ecosocialism Not Extinction
Allan Todd.

Stalinist Realism and Open Communism: Malignant Mirror or Free Association
Ian Parker.

Radical Psychoanalysis and Anti-capitalist Action
Ian Parker.

OTHER POCKET BOOKS

Mind Fuck : The Mass Psychology of Creeping Fascism
Neil Faulkner.

Alienation, Spectacle, and Revolution : A critical Marxist essay
Neil Faulkner.

Why We Need Anti-capitalist Resistance
Simon Hannah.

All titles in the pocket book series are £5 from www.resistancebooks.org.

E-books of these titles are available from online retailers.

Milton Keynes UK
Ingram Content Group UK Ltd.
UKHW022222061223
433909UK00010B/566